Bible Readers Series

A Study of Philippians

JOY IN SERVING CHRIST

Jerald H. Jackson

Abingdon Press / Nashville

JOY IN SERVING CHRIST
A STUDY OF PHILIPPIANS

This book is printed on acid-free paper.

ISBN 0-687-05153-3

ISBN 13: 978-0-687-05153-3

08 09 10 11—10 9 8 7 6 5 4
Manufactured in the United States of America.

CONTENTS

Chapter One

A WORTHY LIFE

PURPOSE

To help us learn how to stand firm in the faith when confronted with opposition

BIBLE PASSAGE

Philippians 1:3-14, 27-30

3 I thank my God every time I remember you, 4 constantly praying with joy in every one of my prayers for all of you, 5 because of your sharing in the gospel from the first day until now. 6 I am confident of this, that the one who began a good work among you will bring it to completion by the day of Jesus Christ. 7 It is right for me to think this way about all of you, because you hold me in your heart, for all of you share in God's grace with me, both in my imprisonment and in the defense and confirmation of the gospel. 8 For God is my witness, how I long for all of you with the compassion of Christ Jesus. 9 And this is my prayer, that your love may overflow more and more with knowledge and full insight 10 to help you to determine what is best, so that in the day of Christ you may be pure and blameless, 11 having produced the harvest of righteousness that comes through Jesus Christ for the glory and praise of God.

12 I want you to know, beloved, that what has happened to me has actually helped to spread the gospel, 13 so that it has become known throughout the whole imperial guard and to everyone else that my imprisonment is for Christ; 14 and most of the brothers and sisters, having been made confident in the Lord by my imprisonment, dare to speak the word with greater boldness and without fear....

27 Only, live your life in a manner worthy of the gospel of Christ, so that, whether I come and see you or am absent and hear about you, I will know that you are standing firm in one spirit, striving side by side with one mind for the faith of the gospel, 28 and are no way intimidated by your opponents. For them this is evidence of their destruction, but of your salvation. And this is God's doing. 29 For he has graciously granted you the privilege not only of believing in Christ, but of suffering for him as well—30 since you are having the same struggle that you saw I had and now hear that I still have.

CORE VERSE
Live your life in a manner worthy of the gospel of Christ.
(Philippians 1:27)

OUR NEED

Writing to Christians in the first century, Paul warned his brothers and sisters in the faith to be ready to face opposition. He understood that those who follow Jesus Christ cannot avoid dealing with conflict, cannot avoid living in tension with the world. Paul wanted his readers to be able to stand firm in their faith.

This tension between the community of faith and the world has not disappeared, even after two thousand years. True, we live in a nation that protects the right of religious expression in its very constitution. But if we dedicate ourselves to living lives that honor Christ, we may find ourselves in conflict with the political, economic, and/or moral powers of our day.

In addition, many Christians face an internal struggle of faith, a struggle to place our lives completely at God's disposal. Paul knew that if a Christian won the internal battle, then he or she would have enough spiritual strength to stand up to external opposition. Paul's example can help us develop this strength. The apostle stood firm in the faith, supported by the companionship of his Christian sisters and brothers. Through reflection on Paul's insight into the spiritual meaning of his suffering, we too can find inspiration, courage, and joy in our Christian lives.

FAITHFUL LIVING

Paul had a special relationship with the Christians in Philippi. This relationship was built on a common bond of faith in Jesus Christ and on shared experiences in proclaiming the gospel.

Like many other contemporary Christians, I long thought of Paul as something of a superstar in the history of the church. I saw him as a daring, charismatic individual, always drawing a crowd, standing alone for his faith, and emerging victorious. But lately I have begun to realize that Paul's reliance on friends was vital to his success.

Paul, then, was like most of us: He recognized that often it is through our companions on life's journey that we gain strength for the tasks of life. These friends share our joys and sorrows; they stand with us when we cannot or do not want to stand alone. Such care for one another is one of the hallmarks of Christian companionship.

In a small town parish I once served, I found many examples of supportive companionship. There was the older woman who lived alone but who assured me, with a sense of peaceful security, "If my neighbor across the street doesn't see my living room shade go up by eight in the morning, she will call or come over to check on me." There was the group at the local cafe, farmers and businesspeople, who would gather to discuss crops and weather, politics and religion. Theirs was a subtle but vibrant sort of companionship. Like Paul, these people relied on friends to help them stand firm in the life of faith.

How has being a companion to others enriched your life?

Experiences That Build Community

Luke speaks of Philippi as "a leading city of the district of Macedonia and a Roman colony" (Acts 16:12). In this important city Paul received an early lesson on the role of friends in helping one stand firm for the faith. We read that Paul angered some who were making a living from "a slave-girl who had a spirit of divination" (Acts 16:16). Paul earned the wrath of the girl's owners by exorcising that spirit, thus removing the owners' source of income. These people took Paul and his companion Silas to court. The punishment meted out against the two Christians was severe: They were stripped, beaten, and thrown into prison (Acts 16:20-24). Only upon learning the two men were Roman citizens did the authorities apologize to them.

In looking back on these events, Paul could recall the friendship and care of the Philippian Christians. They shared with him "from the first day" a common belief in Christ (Philippians 1:5), a belief forged in the heat of opposition. Perhaps nothing binds people together more deeply and more firmly than a communal experience of overcoming difficulties.

A similar pattern of shared experience was a powerful force in shaping the sense of community among early Methodists. Charles Wesley's hymn "And Are We Yet Alive" reflects this joy in overcoming hardships within the bonds of faith:

And are we yet alive,
and see each other's face?
Glory and thanks to Jesus give
for his almighty grace![1]

In verse 3, Wesley speaks of the struggle of faith:

What troubles have we seen,
what mighty conflicts past,
fightings without, and fears within,
since we assembled last![2]

This hymn first appeared in a collection of hymns prepared for Methodists by John Wesley in 1749.[3] The early years of Methodism were anything but serene. The Wesleys were excluded from preaching in the established church, they were beset by unruly mobs, and they were burdened by the physical stress of constant travel on behalf of the gospel. They were no strangers to "fightings without, and fears within." Yet the Wesleys stood firm together in the faith.
How have shared experiences strengthened your faith?

Friends to Count on

Isn't it remarkable that someone under arrest should begin a letter with an expression of thanksgiving? Paul did just that. He thanked God for the witness of his beloved church at Philippi. His Philippian friends knew that he was again a prisoner for the sake of the gospel. Paul was probably in Rome; we read in Acts 21–28 of the circumstances that led up to his being there. During that period of stress, Paul's Christian friends in Philippi responded with material and spiritual support. Through exchange of letters, the apostle and the Philippian Christians kept in contact and comforted one another.

Beneath this account of human readiness to respond to need is a more profound truth: The spiritual health of any one of us is related to our participation in a community of faith. Our spiritual health is strengthened by our having companions and our being a companion to others. That is Paul's secret for standing firm in the faith.

John Wesley was quite sensitive to this fact and structured early Methodist "Bands," "Classes," and "Societies" in such a way as to make it possible for Christians to be supportive of one another. These groups were to meet weekly, the members confessing to one another the temptations they had experienced during the week. In that sharing, they were to find the strength to continue on their journey to perfection.

While the importance of this kind of relationship has been long recognized by students of the Methodist movement, secular historians have also begun to understand the importance the structure had in the success of the movement. As one such historian has written, "The Methodist system of organization encouraged this sense of fellowship. Although the movement was large, the units were small, so that each member felt himself a part of an intimate group."[4] In such fellowship, members "shared a common faith, purpose, and destiny."[5]

Think of the importance of the friends who gather with you to study this chapter. When we join together in our Sunday school classes and Bible study groups, we share in a source of spiritual power that for centuries has enabled Christians to stand firm.

In what ways have you counted on friends in the community of faith?

Deeper Meanings

Paul, like the Old Testament prophets before him, discerned the deeper meaning of events. He shared these spiritual insights with his companions in the faith, including the Philippian Christians. This reflection within community on the deeper meaning of what was happening was a source of strength for Paul and for his readers.

Consider, for instance, how Paul interpreted his imprisonment in his letter to the Philippians. Paul had been arrested in Jerusalem; and after two years of detention, he claimed his rightful day in court before Caesar and was sent to Rome. There Paul began to see how his experience as a prisoner was advancing the cause of the gospel. His imprisonment "for Christ" resulted in an unusual opportunity to preach and teach the Christian message in a pagan world.

This spiritual insight, this "theological" understanding of the events of his life, gave Paul the strength to stand firm. Shared with the Philippians, it helped those Christians deal with the difficulties and obstacles in their own lives.

Paul's faith helped him to see and to seize the opportunity in the moment. His imprisonment gave him the chance to proclaim the gospel to the imperial guard (Philippians 1:13). It was a bold move, but he realized that his example was giving courage to others to proclaim the faith (Philippians 1:14).

We can be confident that Paul would have liked to avoid many of the painful things that happened to him. But through all these experiences, he was governed by an absolute faith that God was able to use any circumstance to complete the divine purpose. This faith reached its most eloquent expression in Paul's letter to the Romans, in which he wrote, "We know that all things work together for good for those who love God, who are called according to his purpose" (Romans 8:28).

Within our Christian communities we see many persons dealing creatively with difficult problems. The strength to stand firm comes from the assurance that God is faithful and that God is able to work creatively even in the worst of circumstances. The witness to faith in the midst of trouble and frustration only helps others to remain firm in their own bad times. Thus Paul offered his suffering as an example to his brothers and sisters in Christ, calling them to live faithfully in their own situation (Philippians 1:27-30).

A marker on the property of a rural church near the village of Hemmingsford Abbots, in East Anglia, England, gives witness to the power of such faith. This country church was built in the midst of the great civil war that shook England in the seventeenth century. The stone marker is a tribute to those who built the church. The marker praises folks who had the courage to do "the best of things, in the worst of times." It is the glory of the church that Christians still give testimony to that profound courage: Christians still do the best of things in the worst of times.

Today, we continue to be vulnerable to moments of doubt (Charles Wesley's "fears within"); few would deny that. We are not able to fit all events neatly into a consistent theological package. Life has many rough edges. Some things simply do not make sense if what we believe about God, made known to us in Jesus Christ, is true. Life will always challenge us to see beneath the events to affirm that God's purpose is still being carried out. Joy comes when we are faithful to the best we know, no matter what the consequences may be. Our friends in the faith, our dear companions, help us see the deeper meaning of our lives; and they help us stand firm.

In what ways do you see the deeper meaning of the events of your life? How does this realization help you to stand firm in "the worst of times"?

> **CLOSING PRAYER**
> Gracious God, grant us an understanding of your holy purpose. Help us to be friends in the faith to one another, companions who give strength and support to one another. Guide us in all we think and do that our lives may reflect your glory. In the name of your Son we pray. Amen.

[1] From "And Are We Yet Alive," in *The United Methodist Hymnal* (Copyright © 1989 by The United Methodist Publishing House); 553.

[2] From "And Are We Yet Alive," in *The United Methodist Hymnal* (Copyright © 1989 by The United Methodist Publishing House); 553.

[3] From *Companion to the Hymnal* (Abingdon Press, 1970); page 90.

[4] From *The Idea of Poverty: England in the Early Industrial Age*, by Gertrude Himmelfarb (Vintage Books, Random House, 1985); page 34.

[5] From *The Idea of Poverty: England in the Early Industrial Age*; page 34.

Chapter Two

CHRIST, OUR MODEL

PURPOSE
To help us recognize that Jesus' servanthood is the model for our life as Christians

BIBLE PASSAGE
Philippians 2:1-16

1 If then there is any encouragement in Christ, any consolation from love, any sharing in the Spirit, any compassion and sympathy, 2 make my joy complete: be of the same mind, having the same love, being in full accord and of one mind. 3 Do nothing from selfish ambition or conceit, but in humility regard others as better than yourselves. 4 Let each of you look not to your own interests, but to the interests of others. 5 Let the same mind be in you that was in Christ Jesus,

> 6 who, though he was in the form
> of God,
> did not regard equality with
> God
> as something to be exploited,
> 7 but emptied himself,
> taking the form of a slave,

being born in human likeness.
And being found in human form,
8   he humbled himself
and became obedient to the
point of death—
even death on a cross.

9 Therefore God also highly exalted him
and gave him the name
that is above every name,
10 so that at the name of Jesus
every knee should bend,
in heaven and on earth and
under the earth,
11 and every tongue should confess
that Jesus Christ is Lord,
to the glory of God the Father.

12 Therefore, my beloved, just as you have always obeyed me, not only in my presence, but much more now in my absence, work out your own salvation with fear and trembling; 13 for it is God who is at work in you, enabling you both to will and to work for his good pleasure.

14 Do all things without murmuring and arguing, 15 so that you may be blameless and innocent, children of God without blemish in the midst of a crooked and perverse generation, in which you shine like stars in the world. 16 It is by your holding fast to the word of life that I can boast on the day of Christ that I did not run in vain or labor in vain.

CORE VERSE
Let the same mind be in you that was in Christ Jesus.
(Philippians 2:5)

OUR NEED

In the first chapter we saw that Paul counseled unity as a way of standing firm when people faced opposition. But the unity of which Paul spoke was not merely an agreement based on compromise. Rather, he envisioned unity *in Christ.* He wrote that the Christian community should be of "the same mind" (Philippians 2:2), the mind of Christ.

This singlemindedness is what gives integrity to the Christian community, what makes Christians different from non-Christians. The uniqueness of the Christian community in our day is preserved only as the Christians who make up the community express the mind or spirit of Jesus Christ in their lives.

We often speak about the importance of role models for young people. But in truth, we never outgrow the need for role models. Every stage of life is a new and unexplored period during which we can benefit from the example of others who have gone before us.

In this chapter we will explore the understanding of servanthood that Paul discovered in the life of Jesus. We will see that Paul lifted the example of Christ as the role model every Christian should emulate.

FAITHFUL LIVING

Read again the opening phrase of this letter: "Paul and Timothy, servants of Christ Jesus" (Philippians 1:1). The word here translated from the Greek as "servants" would have been understood in Paul's time like the word *slaves* is understood today. Paul identified himself and Timothy as slaves of Christ Jesus. This means that Paul made an unconditional commitment to Christ. He "belonged" to Christ, willingly and completely.

Earlier in his life Paul had persecuted the Christian community that gathered after Jesus' death (Galatians 1:13). Paul could not believe that Jesus was the promised Messiah because Paul felt that God would not have made the Anointed

One endure the death of a criminal. Paul reflected on his former attitude when, in the First Letter to the Corinthians, he wrote of the Christian understanding of the Messiah's suffering as a "stumbling block to Jews" (1 Corinthians 1:23). It had truly been a stumbling block for Paul!

But not only for Paul. We recall that the Gospels tell how Jesus taught the disciples that "the Son of Man must undergo great suffering, and be rejected by the elders, the chief priests, and the scribes, and be killed, and after three days rise again" (Mark 8:31). Peter, for one, was upset by this teaching; and, the Scripture says, Jesus "rebuked" him (Mark 8:33). Peter too had much to learn.

And learn he did. The sermon recorded in Acts 2 illustrates Peter's deeper understanding of Jesus' mission. Paul was infuriated by this sort of preaching and sought to punish any who would believe or proclaim such a story. "Breathing threats and murder against the disciples of the Lord" (Acts 9:1), Paul began a career dedicated to the destruction of the church.

Only the appearance of the risen Lord transformed Paul in thought and action. Paul and his brother Pharisees believed that the Messiah would come to establish God's kingdom, not to die on a cross. Paul, however, learned to think of the Messiah in terms of self-giving, sacrifice, and suffering. If Jesus was the Christ, then a whole new ethic was established for those who would follow him: the ethic of the servant.

What people have you known whose lives have been transformed by the power of God?

Jesus, the Incarnate Lord

How is God revealed in the world? Some say we understand what God is like by discovering the order in nature or by appreciating the beauty of the world around us. Others affirm that God is made known to us in the love that we receive from other people. Still others claim that we hear the voice of God in our conscience, an inner sense of what is right. Surely, all these experiences do contribute to our understanding of God.

For Paul, however, the Word of God made flesh in Jesus of Nazareth revealed God to human beings. When Paul wrote of Jesus that he "emptied himself, / taking the form of a slave" (Philippians 2:7), Paul was espousing what Christian theology has called the Incarnation. Paul believed that Jesus dwelt with God before his earthly existence as Jesus of Nazareth. Just as God is eternal, so too is Jesus Christ, who "was in the form of God" (Philippians 2:6).

The human mind reaches its limits in trying to understand the nature and being of God. While we are located in time, we believe that God is eternal. While we *have* a beginning and an end, we believe that God *is* the beginning and the end, "the Alpha and the Omega" (Revelation 21:6).

Paul maintained in the Letter to the Philippians that Jesus also transcended the earthly time that we experience. Paul struggled to find a way to understand Jesus in both human and divine terms. Paul had not seen the Lord during Jesus' earthly ministry; but clearly, the heavenly voice addressing Paul on the Damascus road was that of the risen Christ: "I am Jesus, whom you are persecuting" (Acts 9:5). What an upheaval this was to effect in Paul's life! He would come to recognize God's work in Christ, eventually proclaiming, "In Christ God was reconciling the world to himself" (2 Corinthians 5:19).

During my seminary training this passage from Second Corinthians spoke strongly to my spiritual needs. At that time I was perplexed by the meaning of the Incarnation; the teaching of the church about a triune God was not particularly helpful to me. Then the knowledge; skill; and, yes, the personal faith of my seminary professors brought me to the point where this passage spoke to my heart as well as to my mind. I found that I, like Paul, could discern God working in and through the life, death, and resurrection of Jesus.

Do you have a favorite Scripture passage that expresses the mystery of God's love made known in Jesus Christ? If so, what is it?

Jesus as Our Role Model

Edward Schillebeeckx [SKIL-uh-bakes], the Dutch theologian, begins the introduction to his monumental book *Christ* with an arresting statement: "Jesus, the story of a new life-style."[1] What is that lifestyle? Paul described it as obedience to God; but he realized that Christ offered a new definition of obedience: living the life of a servant. In our Bible Passage, Paul commends this lifestyle to the church at Philippi and to all who would be followers of Jesus.

Remember the portrait of Jesus presented in the Gospels: Jesus challenged the false piety of the Pharisees; he healed sick people in spite of those who believed that the sick deserved their fate; he comforted those who were battered down by the "powers that be"; he made uncomfortable those who were satisfied with themselves; and he preached the good news of the kingdom of God to people rejected by society. Jesus gave perhaps the most vivid example of his mission as servant after his last meal with the disciples when he literally took on the duties of a slave and washed their feet. "I have set you an example, that you also should do as I have done to you" (John 13:15). Jesus the servant changed Paul's life.

Having accepted Jesus as his Lord and Savior, Paul also had to accept this new understanding of obedience. Jesus had been faithful,

obedient to the point of death—
even death on a cross.

(Philippians 2:8)

Paul understood what the first disciples before him had come to understand: God's plan of redemption included suffering. Thus when Paul encountered persecution and suffering at Philippi, he accepted it as an inevitable consequence of his ministry. Paul taught the various communities of faith that he founded, visited, and/or wrote to that Christians should love one another with a self-effacing love. The example of Jesus informed his teaching.

How has the example of Jesus, the servant, touched your life?

The Practice of Faith

Paul gave a simple instruction: "Let each of you look not to your own interests, but to the interests of others" (Philippians 2:4). This is the practical expression of being a servant of Christ. To be concerned about the interests of others is to live the servant role. Certainly, we hear in this an echo of the Golden Rule: "In everything do to others as you would have them do to you; for this is the law and the prophets" (Matthew 7:12).

There is probably no more simple or more profound or more difficult ethical teaching than this. It is one of the first rules of life most of us were taught. If my own experience is any guide, it is a principle we must relearn daily.

When I was a student pastor, a wise layperson told me to remember that some persons are not "easy to love." That comment was her gentle way of reminding me that the special love shared in a Christian community, the love that we know as *agape* [ah-GAH-pay], is redemptive love. That is, *agape* is love extended unconditionally.

Paul (and Jesus before him) called on every Christian to

accept the responsibility of redemptive love within the community of faith. He claimed that it is within our power to live life as a servant of Christ, practicing *agape.*

As every parent knows, children have a tendency to excuse bad behavior by blaming someone else. "He (the other child) made me do it" was a favorite excuse of mine when I tried to justify mistreating my younger brother. If *he* had only behaved differently, then I could have been good. Even as adults we tend to look for excuses to avoid looking "to the interests of others" (Philippians 2:4). But the Christian faith puts the power for this extraordinary ethical behavior right in our own hands. As we acknowledge Jesus Christ as Lord of our lives and commit ourselves to Christian discipleship, the Holy Spirit helps us to live in the manner of Christ, helps us to accept the role of servant. In such a life, we practice our faith, demonstrating that Jesus is our Lord.

Even as Paul counseled self-giving and deference to others, however, he admitted limits to tolerance. As we will see in the next chapter, Paul said there are some who are not to be tolerated, some who are to be strongly resisted (Philippians 3:2). When the integrity of the faith is at stake, Paul would not be indulgent. His warning against "selfish ambition or conceit" (Philippians 2:3) likewise had an assertive connotation. Paul believed that selfish attitudes are destructive to the Christian community and that they weaken its witness to the world. He would not allow such dispositions to flourish in the faith communities with which he had contact.

But are not all our thoughts and actions filled with our own hopes and dreams and needs? Isn't it "natural" for us to think of our own interests first? Aren't we taught to look out for "number one"? How do we overcome these human tendencies? How do we follow Jesus' example and become servants to others? Again, the power lies with the presence of the Spirit; and the power is cultivated in prayer and worship. The fact that Paul found it necessary to write, "Let the same mind be in you that was in Christ Jesus" (Philippians 2:5) implies that he was aware of self-interest among the Philippian Christians. But that he admonished them as a community of faith to follow the example of Christ shows that he believed God could help them to do so. Paul was a realist about life *and* about grace. One of Charles Wesley's hymns expresses a recognition of the conflict within each of us:

> I want a principle within
> of watchful, godly fear,
> a sensibility of sin,
> a pain to feel it near.
> I want the first approach to feel
> of pride or wrong desire,
> to catch the wandering of my will,
> and quench the kindling fire.[2]

May all of us have this watchful, godly fear, so that we may share the mind of Christ and be true servants of God.
How do the spiritual disciplines of prayer and worship help you in the practice of faith?

CLOSING PRAYER
Almighty God, keep us mindful of your Son, Jesus Christ, and the path of obedience he freely chose. Grant us grace through your Holy Spirit to follow his example of true servanthood. In his name we pray. Amen.

---

[1] From *Christ*, by Edward Schillebeeckx, translated by John Bowden (The Crossroad Publishing Company, 1981); page 19.

[2] From "I Want a Principle Within," in *The United Methodist Hymnal* (Copyright © 1989 by The United Methodist Publishing House); 410.

Chapter Three

KEEP ON KEEPING ON

PURPOSE

To help us affirm that we are sustained in our journey of faith by knowing Jesus Christ as Lord

BIBLE PASSAGE

Philippians 3:1-16

1 Finally, my brothers and sisters, rejoice in the Lord. To write the same things to you is not troublesome to me, and for you it is a safeguard.

2 Beware of the dogs, beware of the evil workers, beware of those who mutilate the flesh! 3 For it is we who are the circumcision, who worship in the Spirit of God and boast in Christ Jesus and have no confidence in the flesh— 4 even though I, too, have reason for confidence in the flesh.

If anyone else has reason to be confident in the flesh, I have more: 5 circumcised on the eighth day, a member of the people of Israel, of the tribe of Benjamin, a Hebrew born of Hebrews; as to the law, a Pharisee; 6 as to zeal, a persecutor of the church; as to righteousness under the law, blameless.

7 Yet whatever gains I had, these I have come to regard as loss because of Christ. 8 More than that, I regard every-

thing as loss because of the surpassing value of knowing Christ Jesus my Lord. For his sake I have suffered the loss of all things, and I regard them as rubbish, in order that I may gain Christ 9 and be found in him, not having a righteousness of my own that comes from the law, but one that comes through faith in Christ, the righteousness from God based on faith. 10 I want to know Christ and the power of his resurrection and the sharing of his sufferings by becoming like him in his death, 11 if somehow I may attain the resurrection from the dead.

12 Not that I have already obtained this or have already reached the goal; but I press on to make it my own, because Christ Jesus has made me his own. 13 Beloved, I do not consider that I have made it my own; but this one thing I do: forgetting what lies behind and straining forward to what lies ahead, 14 I press on toward the goal for the prize of the heavenly call of God in Christ Jesus. 15 Let those of us then who are mature be of the same mind; and if you think differently about anything, this too God will reveal to you. 16 Only let us hold fast to what we have attained.

CORE VERSE
I press on toward the goal for the prize of the heavenly call of God in Christ Jesus. (Philippians 3:14)

OUR NEED

How many times have you heard a person say, "That experience made me reorder my priorities"? I understand the point being made. Several years ago a serious illness struck a member of our family. Suddenly, things we had thought were important became insignificant; and schedules we had judged to be essential were set aside. Reminded of the fragility of life, we gained a new perspective. But we did not become discouraged, for we relied on our faith in Jesus Christ for solid footing.

The greatest threat to the faith of the Christian is not opposition from without but discouragement from within. Paul addressed the threat of discouragement when he counseled the Philippians to "rejoice in the Lord" (Philippians 3:1). It is wonderful when we can rejoice in the goodness of life, but Paul reminded his Christian friends that they would also find that God is faithful in the darker moments of life. The key is to "hold fast to what we have attained" (Philippians 3:16). What had they attained? A saving relationship with God through Christ.

In this chapter we will consider how Paul's experience of Jesus Christ changed the way he looked at life and how forgiveness of sins liberated him for service. We will also think about our own journey of faith and the promise that God holds out for us.

FAITHFUL LIVING

In the liturgy of the Lord's Supper of one denomination, they pray that they come to the Lord's Table, "not . . . trusting in our own righteousness, but in thy manifold and great mercies."[1] The alternative to trusting in God is trusting in ourselves and in our own powers. In traditional Protestant theology, this is the difference between *faith* and *works*.

In his earlier life, Paul had felt capable of earning a right relationship with God by keeping the Torah, the Jewish religious law. But in his encounter with Jesus Christ, Paul experienced God's love through trust in Christ. Everything that Paul had previously thought important was set aside. His sense of self-righteousness was banished, and he was given a new vocation.

As we read in Acts 9:15, Paul became God's instrument "whom I have chosen to bring my name before Gentiles and kings and before the people of Israel." As he pursued his calling, seeking to share in Christ's redemptive work, Paul wrote, "I press on to make it my own, because Christ Jesus has made me his own" (Philippians 3:12). Paul's knowledge of Jesus Christ as Lord transformed and energized him. *How has trusting Jesus as Lord transformed your life?*

Our Personal Faith Journeys

Each of us centers his or her life on something we believe to be of vital importance. That center grounds us and gives our life direction. The theologian Paul Tillich spoke of it as that which is of "ultimate concern" to us. The question we must ask is, "Is that ultimate something large enough, deep enough, and challenging enough to satisfy our deepest needs?" Christian faith maintains that only God is great enough to be that center.

Our faith journeys are personal things. Faith is not something we can inherit; we cannot purchase or borrow it; a friend cannot give it to us. To be sure, faith is a gift; but it comes from God, and we must claim it. Nonetheless, in our personal journeys we can find support and strength from others who are pressing on.

When I graduated from college, my father gave me a Bible in which he inscribed the following words: "In 1910 my father gave me a Bible in which he wrote Psalm 1:1-2. I pass it on to you." When my father died in 1972, his theological library came to me. Among those books I found the Bible that he had received from his father. The inscription read, "Presented to Olin Jackson by his Father, Christmas, 1910." Then followed the words of the psalm: "Blessed is the man whose delight is in the Law of the Lord, and on His Law doth he meditate day and night." Those two Bibles, now dog-eared and tattered, stand side by side in my library. They are witnesses to the spiritual companionship I have had throughout my life.

These Bibles have great meaning for me. The fading inscriptions remind me of the fact that the Christian community transcends both space and time. They remind me of a family tradition in which the Word of God and the church have been central. But most important, they remind me that each generation must make the ancient story its own and that each person stands before God and is addressed by God's Word.

This continuity over time is also apparent in the lives of those who worship God. In the various seasons of our lives, we must focus our own faith on that which abides, on that which is ultimate. To confess Jesus Christ as Lord is to make him the center, the ultimate concern of our lives.

What is the center around which your life moves? What is of greatest importance to you?

A Journey Toward the Eternal

Paul began his letter to the Philippians by acknowledging that his position was precarious. He did not know whether he would live or die. Isn't it remarkable that in spite of the dark cloud that was over his head, Paul's attitude was, "I press on" (Philippians 3:12)? He knew that ultimately it did not matter whether he lived or died (Philippians 1:20-24). What did matter was that he remain committed to the "prize of the heavenly call of God in Christ Jesus" (Philippians 3:14). Paul was focused on Christ; his life was in the hands of God.

Paul could put his life at risk because he believed that death does not end our spiritual journey, that death is not the final chapter. As he was to write with such eloquence to the Romans, "I am convinced that neither death, nor life, nor angels, nor rulers, nor things present, nor things to come, nor powers, nor height, nor depth, nor anything else in all creation, will be able to separate us from the love of God in Christ Jesus our Lord" (Romans 8:38-39). Paul taught that the Christian's destiny is to be united with Christ in love forever.

Paul's declaration in Romans reminds us that we are being drawn toward a future that God is preparing. We are participating in a divine plan, having been called by God. No matter what our age, our experience, our education, or our circumstances may be, God acts to sustain us in our efforts to respond to that call. Our belief in Christ as Lord of this life and of the life to come—not a mere intellectual assent but a heartfelt trust in God's goodness—enables us to continue in our journey of faith.

How does faith in God's gift of eternal life affect the way you live?

Let Your Light So Shine

We all find it is so easy to slip into patterns of thought that minimize our individual importance. So many things seem to be beyond our personal control. Has God actually called us to some work? Can we really make any difference in the world? These questions troubled people in biblical times, too. In the Scriptures we find many examples of people who protested that they were not the right person to carry out God's will. For instance, Moses protested when God called him to be the instrument of release for the Israelites: "Who am I that I should go to Pharaoh, and bring the Israelites out of Egypt?" (Exodus 3:11).

The Bible also offers many examples of rather ordinary people who accomplished great things through faith in God. Certainly, the transformation of the disciples from frightened, confused, tentative followers of Jesus to assured proclaimers of the faith is an inspiring record. Still, that each one of us has a special role to play in the story of salvation may be the most difficult element of faith to take as one's own. We are so strongly influenced by secular values that we are tempted to accept what the world defines as "really important" as, well, really important. During the past few years there has been a persistent emphasis on the unequaled value of youth. This cultural emphasis has been so strong that older people sometimes feel useless. As a pastor, I have had many older persons speak of this feeling to me. They wonder why they are still alive; they feel pushed out of the mainstream of life; they are discouraged. Yet all of them, even those who are homebound, are at important crossroads on their spiritual journey.

Consider these examples: One of these older persons is able to be a source of strength and comfort for her daughter who is going through a difficult divorce. Another gives countless hours of strength and companionship to grandchildren who will remember and cherish the gifts of their grandfather for the rest of their lives. Another helps organize the church prayer chain that provides the spiritual cement for a scattered, urban congregation.

I recall one parishioner, whom I will call Mary, who exhibited the greatest courage in the face of overwhelming problems. Mary had had a relatively normal life. She had married and eventually brought two children into the world. She had much for which to be grateful and even more to look forward to. But then, when Mary was in her late twenties, she was stricken with polio. She lost the use of her arms and legs and was confined to an iron lung machine for breathing support. By the time I met Mary, she had lived in an iron lung for more than twenty years.

But Mary *had lived well*. She had taught herself to paint, holding the brush between her teeth. She proudly gave me one of her paintings. Mary had also become involved with a rehabilitation center in our community and had been appointed the associate administrator. Because of her physical condition, she had every reason to feel useless; and perhaps there were moments when she did. But though Mary's body was severely limited, her spirit was undefeated. I will always remember the lesson she taught me by her example of courage, hope, and vitality. Mary led an active life centered on her trust in Jesus Christ as Lord. Like Paul, she pressed on toward the goal.

How have you dealt with feelings of uselessness or helplessness?

Forgetting and Remembering

If we are to make the best of this journey of faith, we need to be selective about what we take along. There were some things Paul needed to forget, and there were some things he needed to remember. In a short space, Paul wrote of both: "Forgetting what lies behind" (Philippians 3:13) and "hold[ing] fast to what we have attained" (Philippians 3:16). Forgetting and remembering are both important.

I have served several churches as pastor and held a conference office in the years since my seminary days. Each time our family is called upon to go to a new assignment, we know we must leave behind many things that we hold dear and many people whom we love. We have never found this easy. But, while we should not forget the wonderful people and experiences of the past, in a way they must be left behind. We cannot seize the new opportunities unless we are in some way free from the old.

Paul Tillich once wrote, "Life could not continue without throwing the past into the past."[2] Implied in Tillich's comment is the understanding that life is supposed to move forward. We are intended to press on. If we have made mistakes, if we have caused hurt, if we have not lived up to the best we know, these things must be forgotten. That is the meaning of the forgiveness that is possible through knowing Jesus Christ. Paul could in an important sense "forget" his past as a persecutor of the church (although, of course, his letters show that he remembered it well) because he had experienced God's forgiving love; that is, he knew Jesus Christ. What Paul gladly "threw into the past" was the life he lived before he met Jesus. That to which Paul held fast was "the surpassing value of knowing Christ Jesus my Lord" (Philippians 3:8). Like Paul, we can be uplifted in our faith journey by knowing Jesus Christ in our own lives.

Are there things in your past you need to discard before you can move ahead in your spiritual journey? If so, what are they?

CLOSING PRAYER
Dear God, we joyfully open our hearts to your grace, seeking your saving presence in our faith journey. Help us to focus on the love of Christ and on the call to his service. In Jesus' name we pray. Amen.

---

[1] From "The Order for the Administration of the Sacrament of the Lord's Supper or Holy Communion," in *The Book of Worship* (Copyright © 1964, 1965 by Board of Publication of The Methodist Church, Inc.); page 23.

[2] From *The Eternal Now,* by Paul Tillich (Charles Scribner's Sons, 1963); page 27.

Chapter Four

REJOICE IN THE LORD

PURPOSE
To encourage us to rejoice in the power of God to satisfy our needs

BIBLE PASSAGE

Philippians 4:4-20

4 Rejoice in the Lord always; again I will say, Rejoice. 5 Let your gentleness be known to everyone. The Lord is near. 6 Do not worry about anything, but in everything by prayer and supplication with thanksgiving let your requests be made known to God. 7 And the peace of God, which surpasses all understanding, will guard your hearts and your minds in Christ Jesus.

8 Finally, beloved, whatever is true, whatever is honorable, whatever is just, whatever is pure, whatever is pleasing, whatever is commendable, if there is any excellence and if there is anything worthy of praise, think about these things. 9 Keep on doing the things that you have learned and received and heard and seen in me, and the God of peace will be with you. 10 I rejoice in the Lord greatly that now at last you have

revived your concern for me; indeed, you were concerned for me, but had no opportunity to show it. 11 Not that I am referring to being in need; for I have learned to be content with whatever I have. 12 I know what it is to have little, and I know what it is to have plenty. In any and all circumstances I have learned the secret of being well-fed and of going hungry, of having plenty and of being in need. 13 I can do all things through him who strengthens me. 14 In any case, it was kind of you to share my distress.

15 You Philippians indeed know that in the early days of the gospel, when I left Macedonia, no church shared with me in the matter of giving and receiving, except you alone. 16 For even when I was in Thessalonica, you sent me help for my needs more than once. 17 Not that I seek the gift, but I seek the profit that accumulates to your account. 18 I have been paid in full and have more than enough; I am fully satisfied, now that I have received from Epaphroditus the gifts you sent, a fragrant offering, a sacrifice acceptable and pleasing to God. 19 And my God will fully satisfy every need of yours according to his riches in glory in Christ Jesus. 20 To our God and Father be glory forever and ever. Amen.

> **CORE VERSE**
> *Rejoice in the Lord always; again I will say, Rejoice.*
> *(Philippians 4:4)*

OUR NEED

An old saying tells us that certain things cannot be taught, they can only be learned. For example, we all want to protect others from making mistakes; but learning often comes precisely from making mistakes. There is, after all, no substitute for experience.

We may, of course, try to pass along something we have learned from our experience by offering advice to another. Although such advice is seldom appreciated, we should testify to that which has strengthened us and has seen us through hard times. After all, our observations are part of the collective wisdom of humankind.

In this lesson we will eavesdrop, so to speak, on Paul's advice to the Christians at Philippi. Paul gave witness to his experience and promised that the strength he found was available to any who were open to receive it. Paul could say, "I have learned to be content with whatever I have" (Philippians 4:11). We will see how Paul learned to trust in God's providence through his suffering for Christ. Paul's exhortation to joy carried weight with the Philippians, for Paul's experience allowed him to speak with an authority that rang true.

FAITHFUL LIVING

The world is full of people who claim to have authority. We hear much advice from those who want to affect our lives. What we look for is someone who speaks with *authentic* authority.

We are—and we should be—wary of those who present themselves as authorities. But we welcome a person who has demonstrated the right to share advice because he or she has undertaken a discipline of study, has passed the test of time, and has proved to be effective.

The apostle Paul was such a person. When he felt it appropriate, Paul did not hesitate to remind his readers that his knowledge was well founded. He recounted in his first letter to the Corinthians that he stood among those who had firsthand experience of the risen Lord: "Last of all, as to one untimely born, he appeared also to me" (1 Corinthians 15:8). The gospel Paul preached was not something he received secondhand.

In addition, Paul had long experience as a missionary and

preacher of the gospel. We read in Acts 13 that Paul was "set apart" (Acts 13:2), along with Barnabas, by the church at Antioch for a special ministry because of his unique gifts and graces. Paul's commission came only after he was able to prove himself to the church—first to Ananias and to other followers in Damascus (Acts 9:10-22), then to the disciples in Jerusalem (Acts 9:26-30), and finally to those in the church at Antioch (Acts 11:25-26).

Paul could also point to the suffering he had endured in his ministry as an authentication of his authority. He bore the marks of his faithfulness to Jesus in his body (Galatians 6:17). He reminded the Christians at Corinth of the hardships he endured: "Five times I have received from the Jews the forty lashes minus one. Three times I was beaten with rods. Once I received a stoning. Three times I was shipwrecked; for a night and a day I was adrift at sea" (2 Corinthians 11:24-25). Paul used these experiences to give credence to this witness.

Finally, Paul could cite the effectiveness of his ministry. His preaching had borne fruit: Many had been converted to faith in Jesus Christ. That too was a source of authority, for it demonstrated the power of God that worked through his ministry.

For all these reasons, Paul felt he had earned the right to give advice to his brothers and sisters in the faith. The centuries have proved that Paul did indeed speak with authentic authority.

To whom do you turn for spiritual advice? Why?

Trust Rooted in Experience

Paul's advice was grounded in his own experience of the presence and power of God. Out of this he offered the antidote to worry—trust in God. Listen to the reassuring words he offered in this last section of the Letter to the Philippians: "The Lord is near" (Philippians 4:5b). "The peace of God . . . will guard your hearts . . . and the God of peace will be with you" (Philippians 4:7, 9). "My God will fully satisfy every need of yours" (Philippians 4:19). These are words of comfort and encouragement that come from years of faithful service.

Never once did Paul complain to or argue with God about the hardships he had endured. He did pray that a particular ailment that he called a "thorn . . . in the flesh" might be removed (2 Corinthians 12:7b-9). But he eventually accepted the "thorn" as a divine lesson in humility. Paul understood that God does not remove all hardship, but God does see people through all hardship; and Paul's trust in God deepened.

It may seem a difficult truth; but unless we have endured hardship, we do not have the depth of experience that brings trust in God. Paul said, "In any and all circumstances I have learned the secret of being well-fed and of going hungry, of having plenty and of being in need" (Philippians 4:12b). What is that secret? "I can do all things through him who strengthens me" (4:13).

Occasionally, we find a basic event in life that seems to express our need to experience life's challenges. For me it came one warm June day as I stood on the south rim of the Grand Canyon, marveling at that remarkable sight. I recall thinking how exciting it would be to hike to the bottom. But my next thoughts were, *No, it's too far; it's too deep. I am too old and too out of shape.* Yet that canyon would not let go of me, and before long a friend and I were planning to make the hike.

After several months of preparation and training (including a good deal of walking), we set out. The final thousand feet of the descent were excruciatingly painful. I never knew that going downhill could be so difficult. That evening I sat soaking my legs in the cold water of Bright

Angel Creek, reveling in the satisfaction of having completed the trip down. Early the next morning I joined my friend on Bright Angel trail to begin the nine-mile climb back to the rim. We were a sorry sight when we finally made it up. But we did make it.

My Grand Canyon experience has been an important event for me, serving as a metaphor for the challenges of life. We do not know what we can do until we make the effort, knowing full well the risks involved. Now when I face a difficult task and am tempted to think it is beyond my strength, I remember the Grand Canyon. When facing a daunting spiritual task, I have the added confidence of knowing that the God who has supported me in the past is near in the present.

Have you faced challenges that demanded more of you than you felt you were capable of doing? If so, what were the circumstances?

Habits of the Heart

What Paul learned from a life of service to his Lord was that the Christian can strengthen his or her spirit by cultivating some habits of the heart. When Paul called on his readers to "rejoice in the Lord always" (Philippians 4:4), he was recommending a habit of the heart: joyfulness. When he suggested, "By prayer and supplication with thanksgiving let your requests be made known to God" (Philippians 4:6), he was encouraging a habit of the heart: prayerfulness. When he said, "Keep on doing the things that you have learned and received and heard and seen" (Philippians 4:9), he was giving testimony to a proven habit of the heart: faithfulness.

Let us look in more detail at how Paul advised Christians to cultivate these habits. First, Paul urged his readers to "rejoice in the Lord" (Philippians 4:4). We might rephrase that as, Express the joy you have because you are the Lord's. The Christian can rejoice in the Lord "in any and all circumstances" (Philippians 4:12) because of the blessing of salvation. Nothing else can compare with this gift. If we glance back to the closing verses of the third chapter of Philippians, we see why Paul knows this to be true. There he described the Christians as having a new, heavenly citizenship (Philippians 3:20). Believing in this promise of heaven, the Christian can joyfully cope with anything.

If joyfulness is to become a habit of the heart, we need to practice rejoicing. The psalmist declared, "This is the day that the LORD has made; / let us rejoice and be glad in it" (Psalm 118:24). We often experience the joy of Christian life while worshiping with other Christians. Worship can form and shape our hearts toward joy so that we can respond as Christians to any situation.

I cannot count the number of times when worshiping with a congregation has enabled me to "rejoice" when I felt less than joyful. Singing the great hymns of faith, hearing the Word read and interpreted, praying with the congregation—all these activities fortify us in the trials of life. We cannot grow spiritually unless we take Paul's advice and express our joy in knowing Christ Jesus.

Second, Paul offered reassurance that God was actively present in the lives of the Philippians, always accessible in prayer. Paul wrote that God is near; therefore "do not worry about anything, but in everything by prayer ... let your requests be made known to God" (Philippians 4:6). Paul's witness reiterated what Jesus taught his disciples when he said, "Ask, and it will be given you; search, and you will find; knock, and the door will be opened for you" (Luke 11:9).

For most of us this kind of trusting approach to prayer reflects a level of spiritual maturity for which we still strive. Especially when we see many persons left destitute through catastrophic illnesses or loss of employment, we cannot help but wonder, "Will I have enough to see me through?" But as we practice bringing our needs before God in prayer, we are cultivating a habit of the heart. The discipline of prayer nurtures our sense of trust in God's care and contributes to our spiritual growth.

Third, Paul commended the practice of faithfulness. He urged his Philippian readers, in effect, to keep on keeping on (Philippians 4:9). Paul's own life was a record of such fidelity. In good times and in bad, in triumph and in defeat, in celebration and in incarceration, Paul testified to the love of God revealed in Jesus Christ. For generations, Paul's counsel has helped nourish the habit of faithfulness in Christians—ordinary folks who in the ebb and flow of their lives remain constant in their affection for an obedience to God. These anonymous Christians are truly extraordinary, for they have constructed lives centered on discipleship. By keeping on keeping on, they have fostered the habit of faithfulness.

What "habits of the heart" have you cultivated?

Words of Appreciation

Paul did not forget to thank the Philippians for the gifts that Epaphroditus [i-paf-ruh-DI-tuhs] brought to him on their behalf (Philippians 4:18). Paul marveled at their generosity and readily commended the Philippian congregation to other churches as an example worthy of following. He wrote these words to the church at Corinth: "For, as I can testify, they [the Philippians] voluntarily gave according to their means, and even beyond their means, begging us earnestly for the privilege of sharing in this ministry to the saints" (2 Corinthians 8:3-4).

Here we see the marks of Christian generosity: Giving is voluntary, coming from an inner disposition toward giving in response to the immeasurable gift that God has given us in Christ. Giving is in accordance with our means, as God has prospered us. Giving is a privilege for us, for it gives us opportunity to participate in the ministry of our brothers and sisters in Christ.

While Paul is grateful for the gifts, he is more grateful for the attitude that motivates the giving: one of stewardship. The very word *stewardship* implies responsibility. The steward is one who has been given responsibility for the affairs of another; and to fulfill that assignment, the steward will act in harmony with the will of the owner. Paul understood that all things of this world were gifts of God and that the good steward would use those gifts in ways that fulfilled God's purposes.

Moreover, it was not simply that Paul needed the support given by the church at Philippi. Rather, the Philippian Christians needed to make the gift, if not to Paul, then to someone else.

In our time we often turn the spiritual meaning of generosity around. We concentrate on the external need to be met and forget the internal need to give. When Jesus observed the generosity of the widow—one who gave "out of her poverty"—he helped us to see how important giving is in Christian living (Luke 21:1-4).

Supporting the church and giving to others are not burdens imposed from without but opportunities sensed from within. Paul quoted Jesus as saying, "It is more blessed to give than to receive" (Acts 20:35). Paul had learned what he in turn would teach: Through participating in God's word to meet the needs of others, we have further occasion to rejoice.

How has giving been an occasion of joy for you?

CLOSING PRAYER
Almighty and compassionate God, we rejoice in your power to meet our needs. Help us cultivate holy habits of the heart, putting our trust in your abundant love. In Jesus' name we pray. Amen.
